F**k Off, I'm 50

By Tara West

With Illustrations
By Leena Cruz

To Bam, who will never reach this milestone.

To cancer. Fuck off!

To Deb, for supporting me along the way
and the "anal probe."

To my lovely moddess goddesses, for your humanity,
intelligence, determination, and kindness,
and for inspiring me to be a better person.

And finally, to Leena. Thank you so much
for bringing my crazy ideas to life!
I'm amazed by your talent. You rock!!!

F**k Off, I'm 50

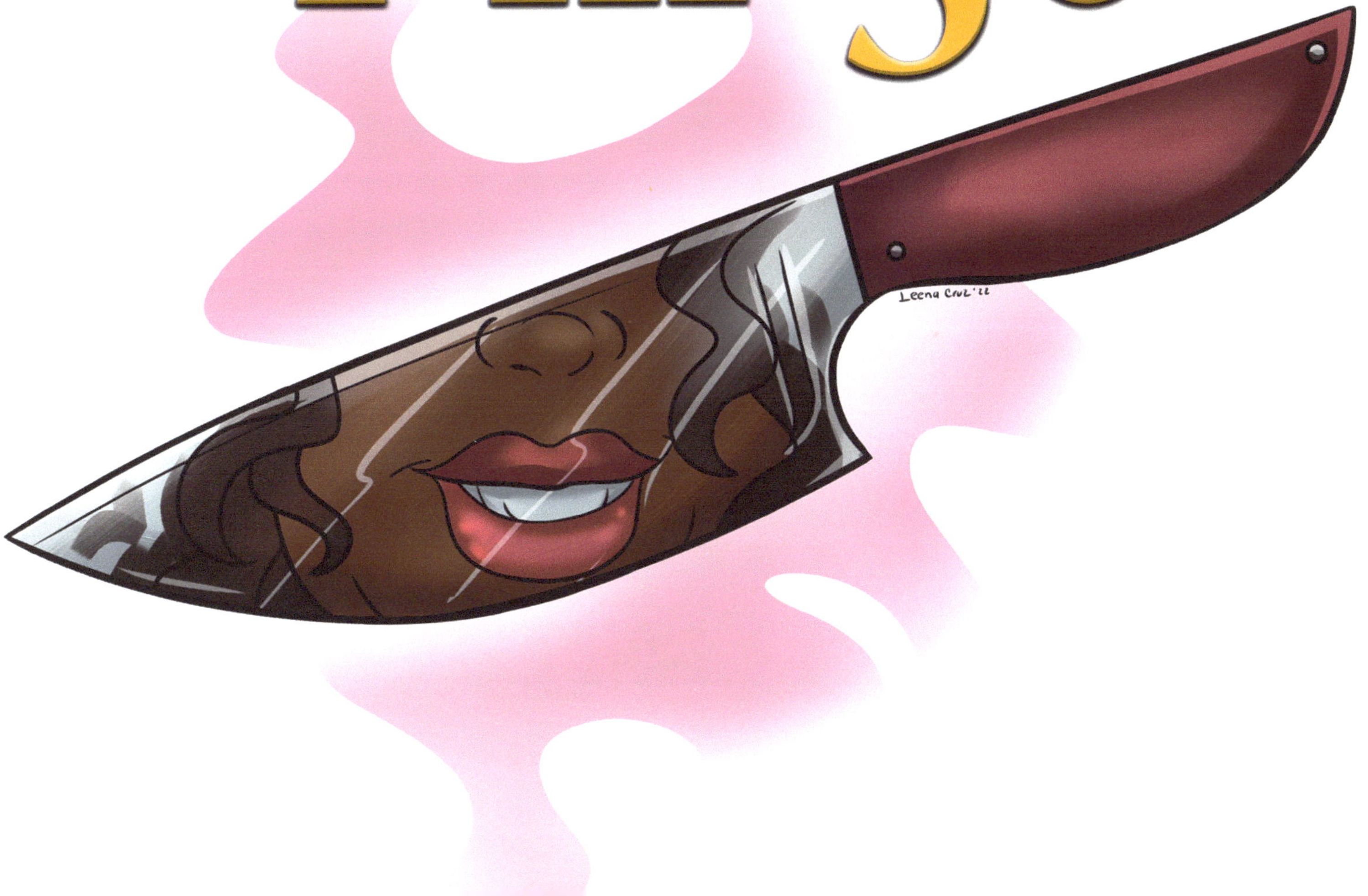

Leena Cruz'22

Hey, you, muffin top,
proudly coming up for air.
I could hide you with a puffy shirt
or find something else to wear.

But the fact
of the matter is
I
just
don't
care.

Bring on the yoga pants
and messy hair.
I still think they're nifty.

And to anyone who doesn't like it, fuck off, I'm 50.

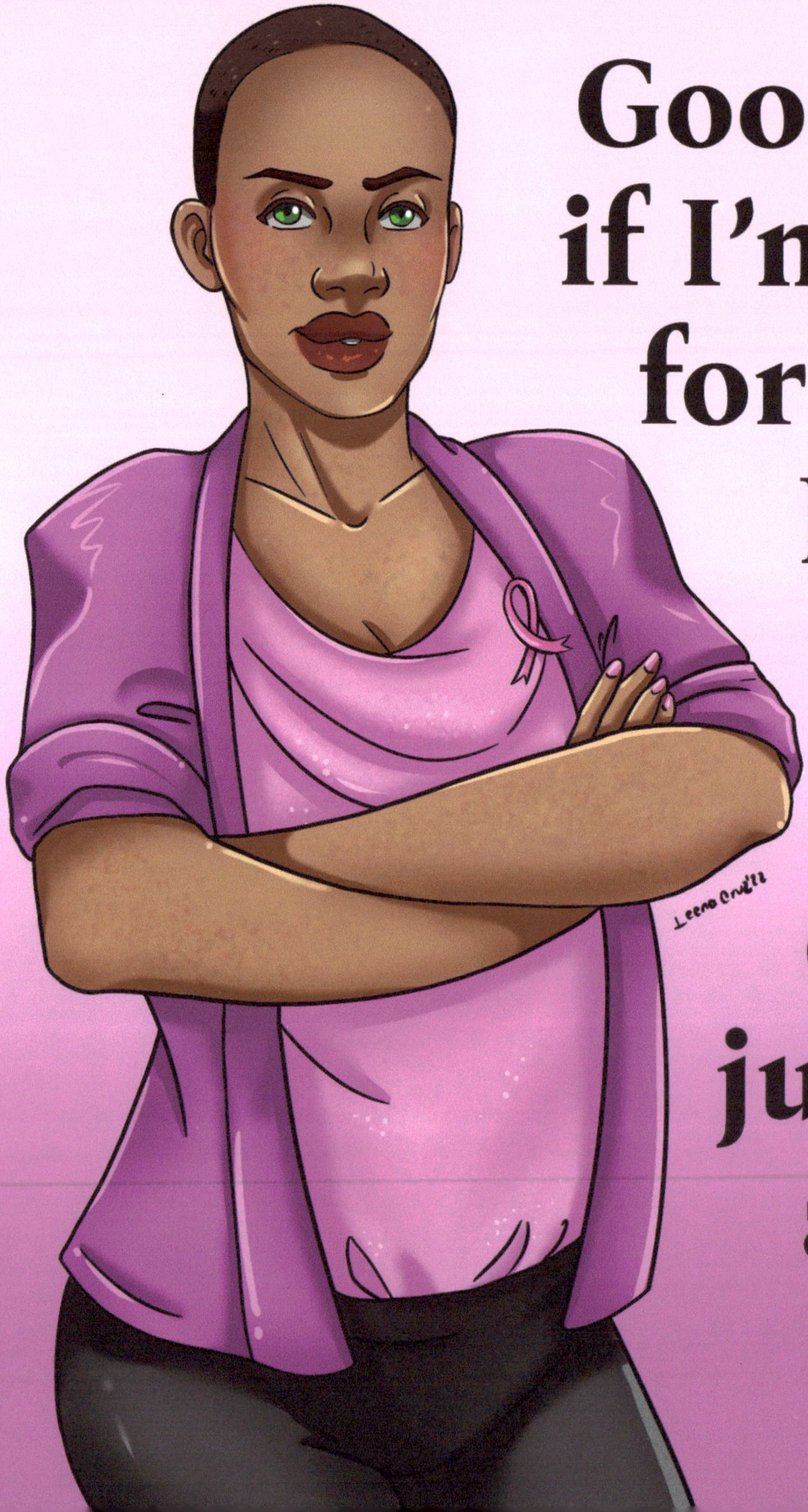

Goodbye worrying
if I'm good enough
for the position.
Instead of
telling me
how to
do my job,
just sit there
and listen.

Or don't.
See if I care.
You don't know
what
you're
missing.

I work twice as hard
and complain half as much
while everyone else worries
about feelings and such.

And if you think my resume looks iffy, fuck off, I'm 50.

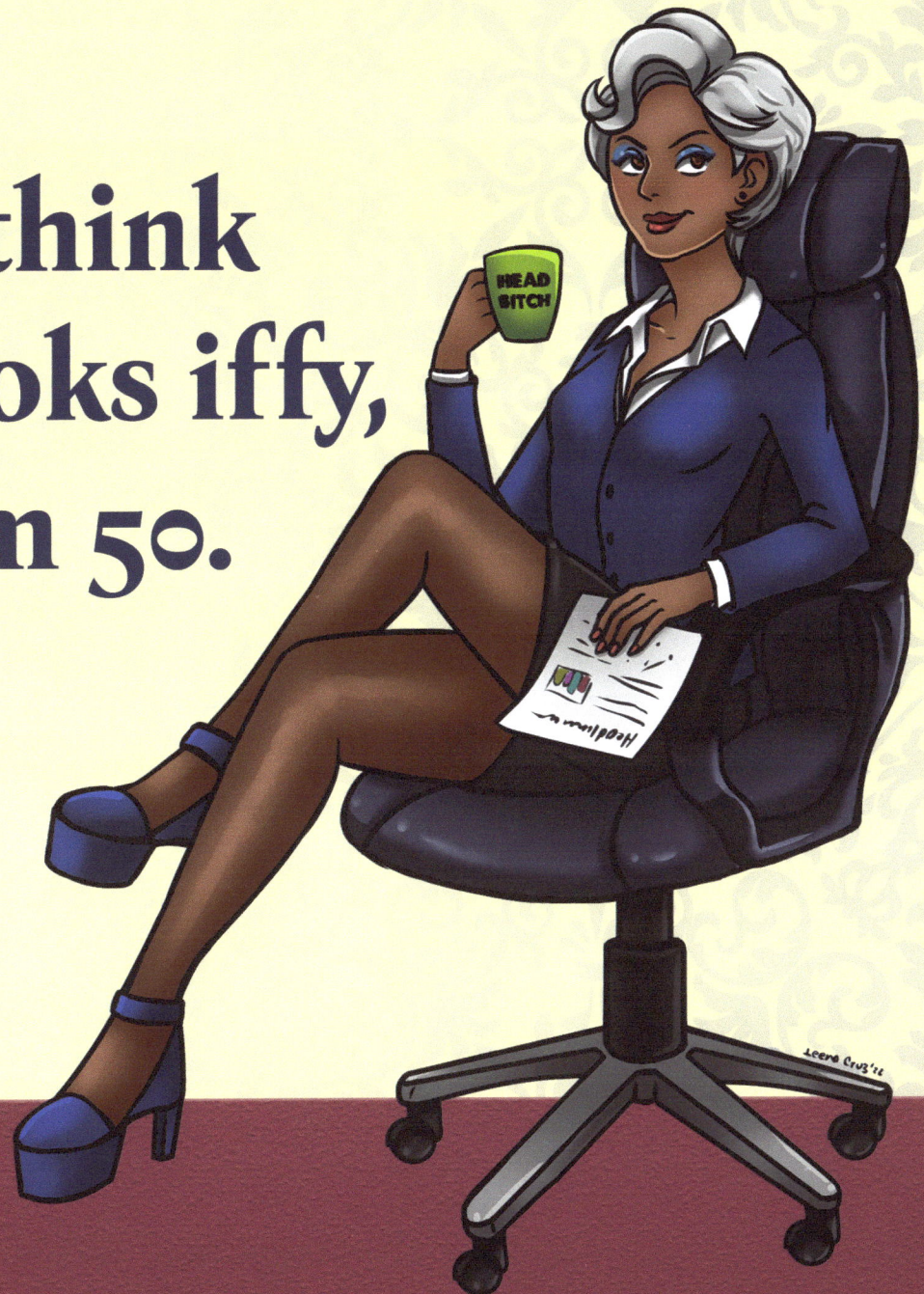

Now that my soul is wiser
after dealing with years of strife,
save a prayer, dearly beloved,
I've survived this thing called life.

I will not be a rainbow
in the dark.
I will not be afraid
of the sun.
I will not hide
who I am inside,
because goddesses
just want to have fun.

So hit me with your best shot, but you'd better not miss.

I'm fucking 50 and will cut you like a knife, then seal it with a kiss.

How could I forget
my Exes and old lovers?
After all,
we shared some fun

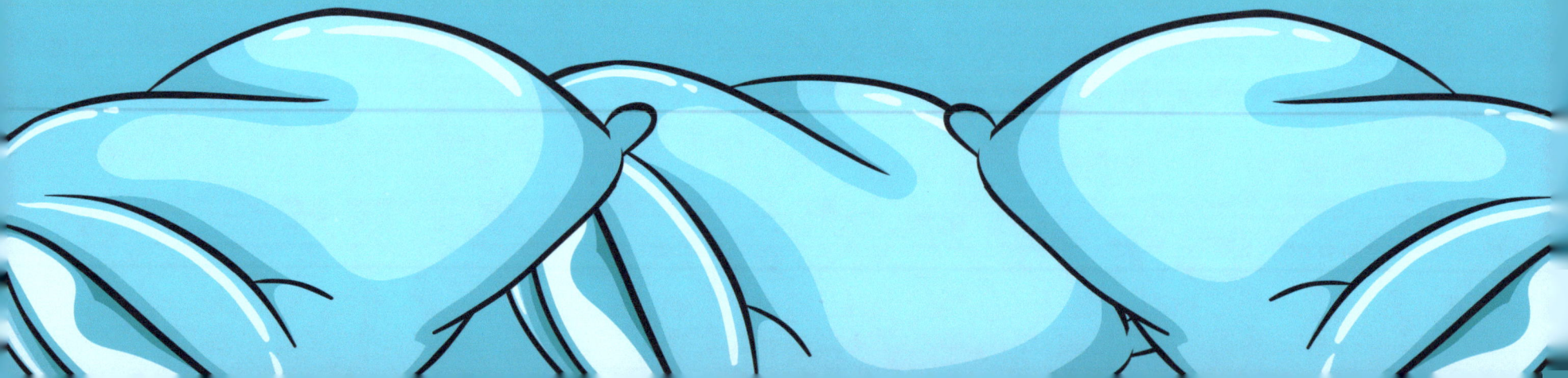

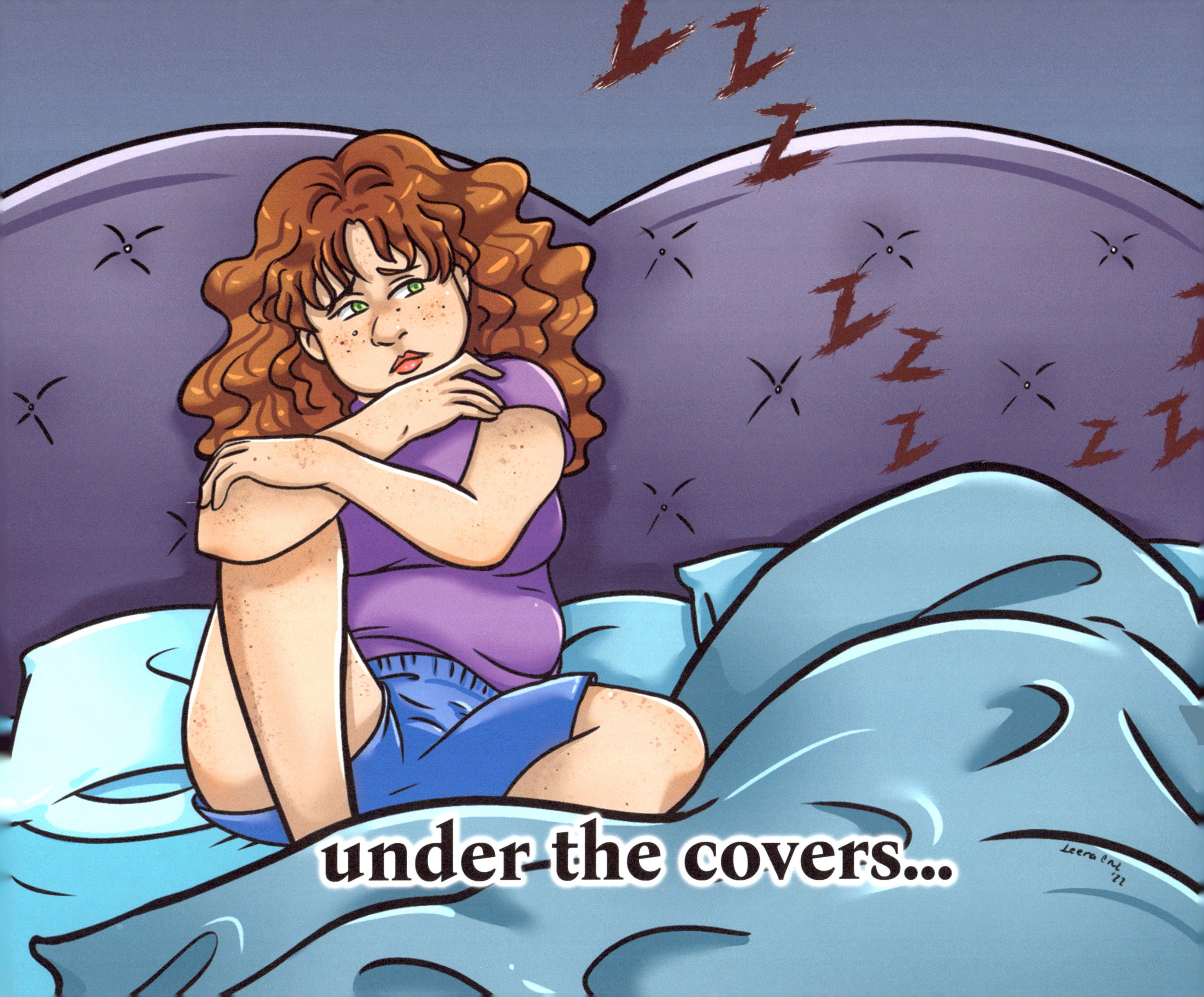
under the covers...

But I'm no longer that naïve girl you knew. Things have changed. You're old shoe.

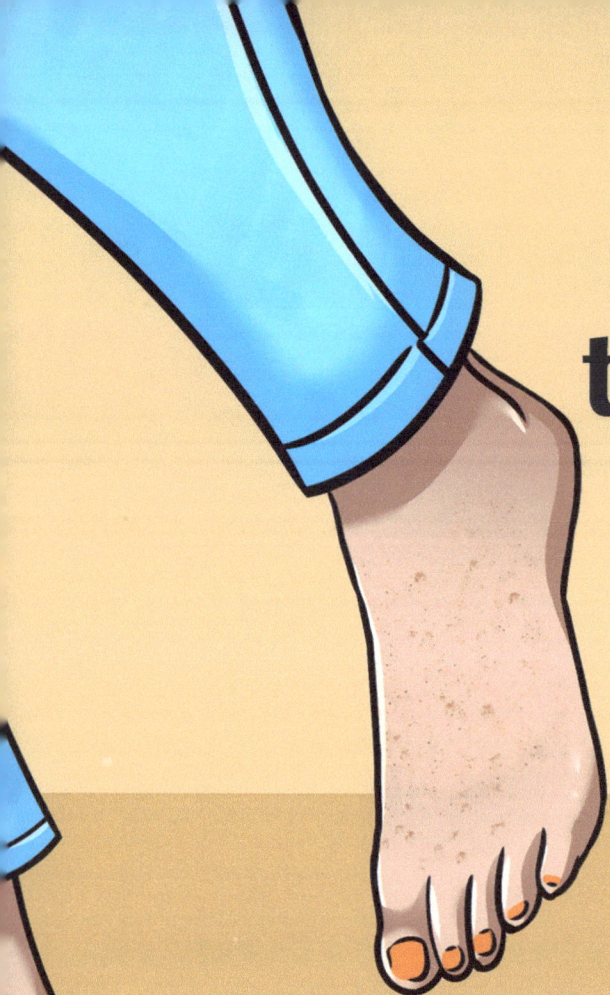

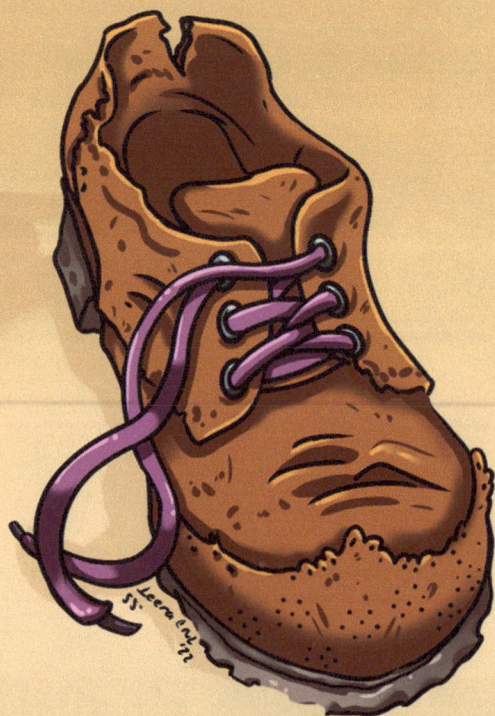

So I hope you're not holding your breath.

Fuck off.
It's too late
for regrets.

I practiced cold war drills,
stayed home alone,
and then made TV dinners.

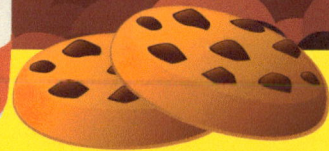

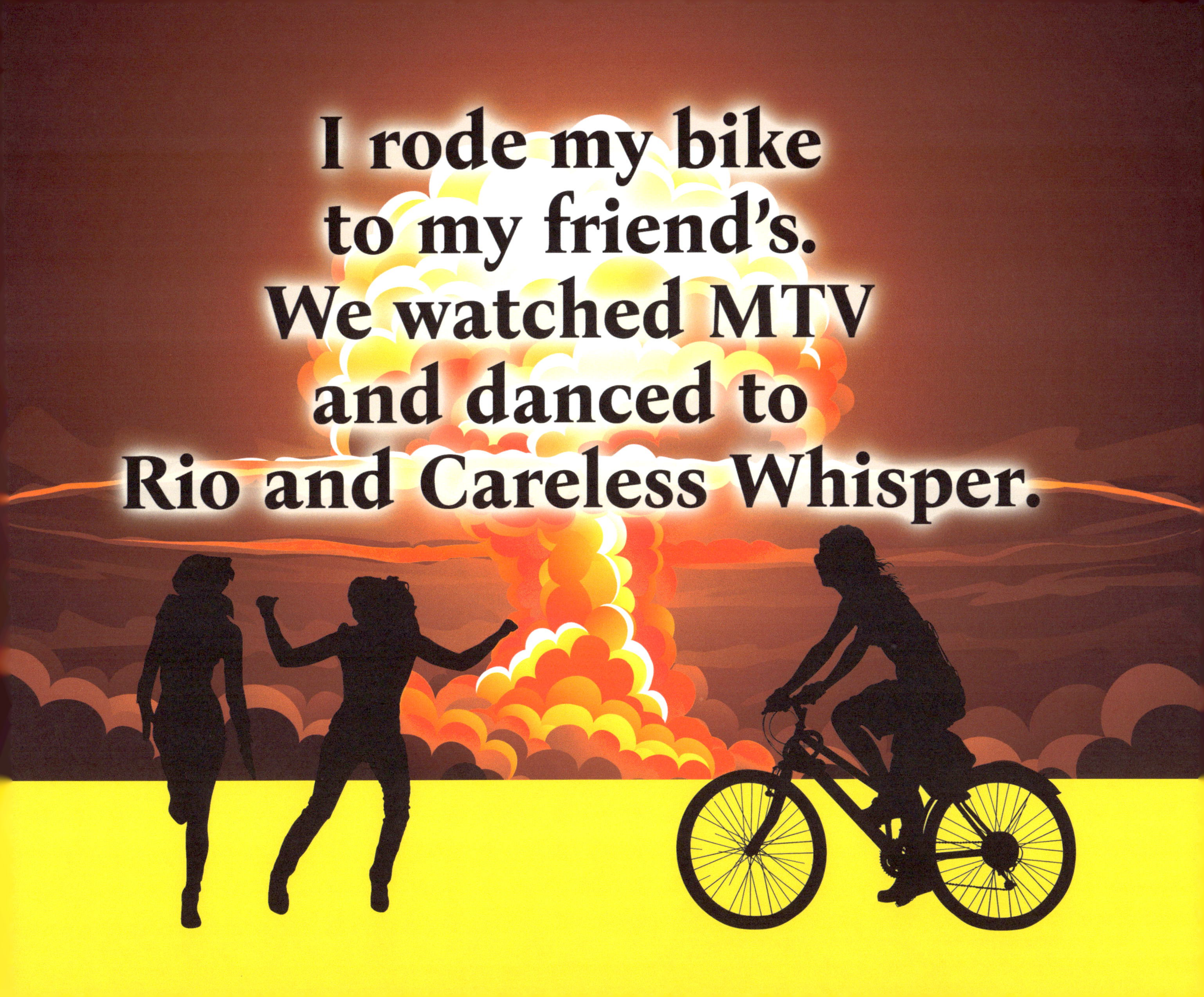

I rode my bike
to my friend's.
We watched MTV
and danced to
Rio and Careless Whisper.

I babysat
the neighbor's kids
and belted my
high-rise jeans.
Then I teased and
sprayed my hair
until it scraped
the ceiling beams.

I flipped burgers after school while keeping up my grades. And if you think my shoulder pads weren't cool, go suck a rotten egg.

Go ahead and laugh
at my letter in the mail.
I'll enjoy my discounts,
and you can go to hell.
I'm not too old to work
and pay the rent.

Just don't come crying when your money's all been spent

Because, guess what? You're not borrowing a cent.

Why?
I'm 50,
and you can
go
get
bent.

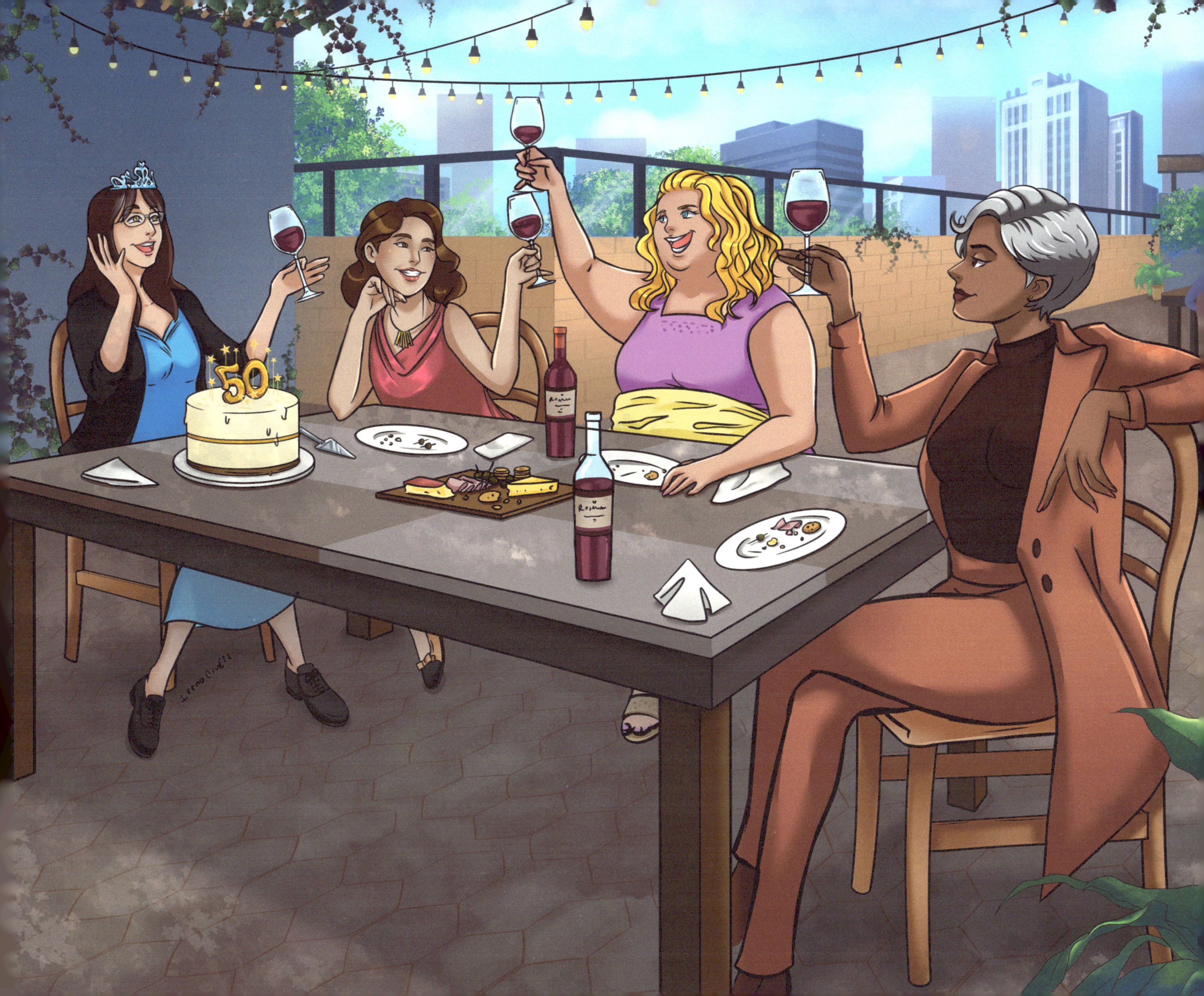
50

Two-faced family
and fake friends,
this is where
our road ends.

I've had enough,
that's it!
I'm not putting up
with your shit.

Life's too short
to get stuck
on memory lane.

Fuck off
far away from me
and let me off
your crazy train.

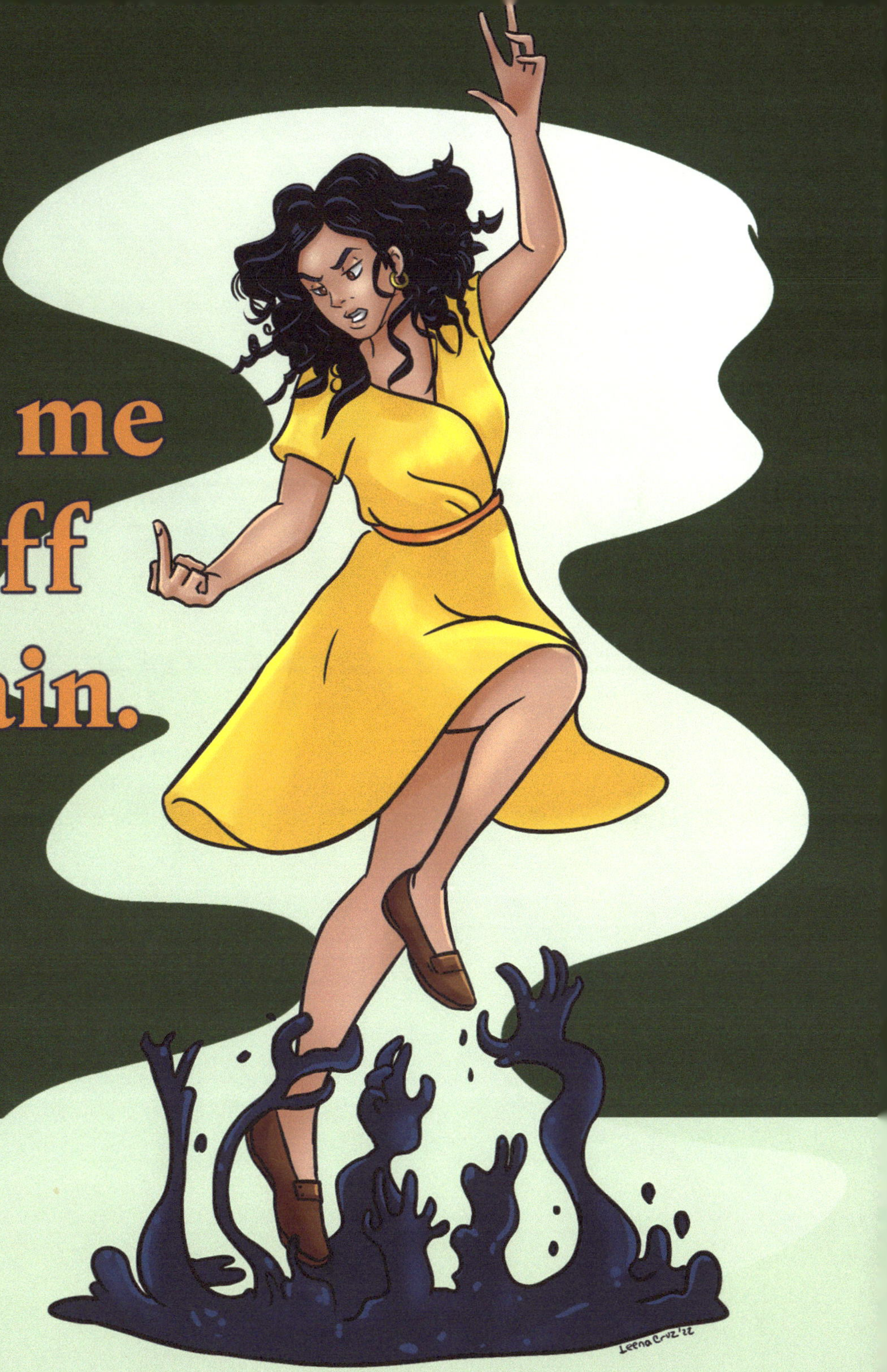
Leena Cruz '22

Step back condescending shamers of the world. When will you realize I'm not a little girl?

I was fierce at forty, but I'm ferocious at 50, and there's more still to come.

So move over, Rover, and let this queen take over.

Fuck off
until I’m done.

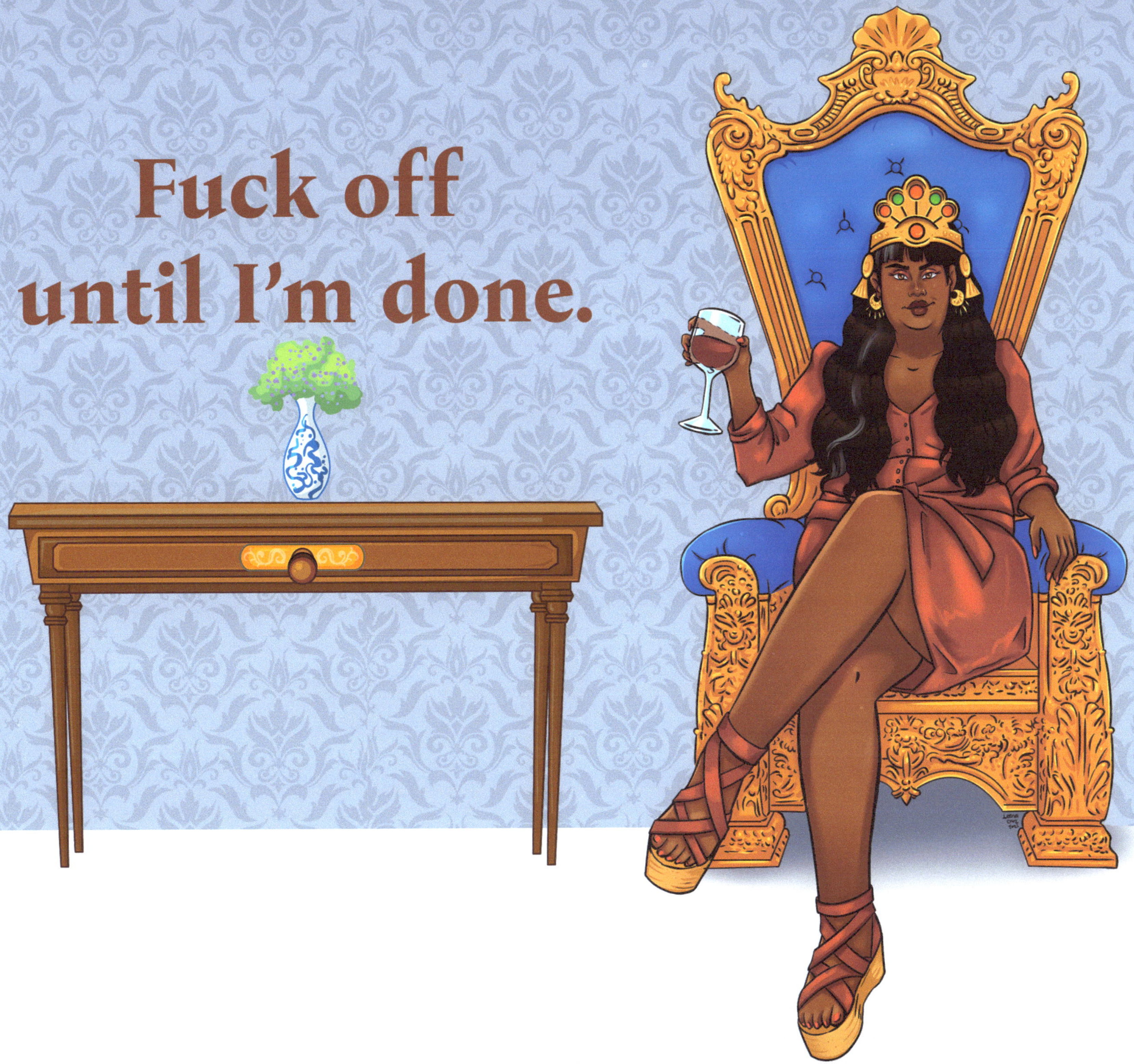

Party all night
means in bed by ten.
I need my sleep,
or I lose my zen.

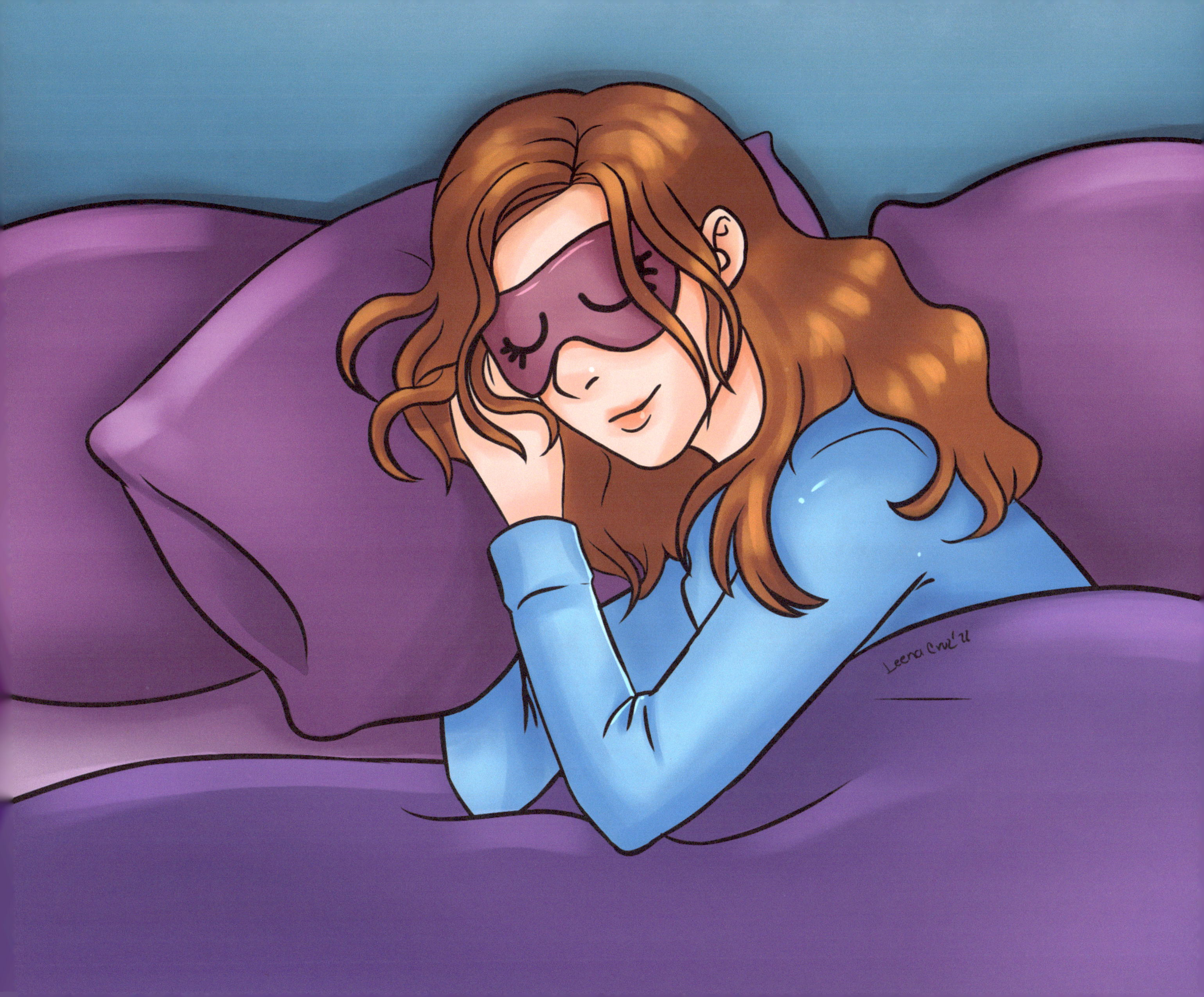
Leena

Another cup of brew?
It's okay by me,
as long as I don't sneeze
when I have to pee.
Carbs? No, thanks.
Well, maybe a small slice.

Aw, fuck it,
I'm 50.
I'll take
the whole pie.

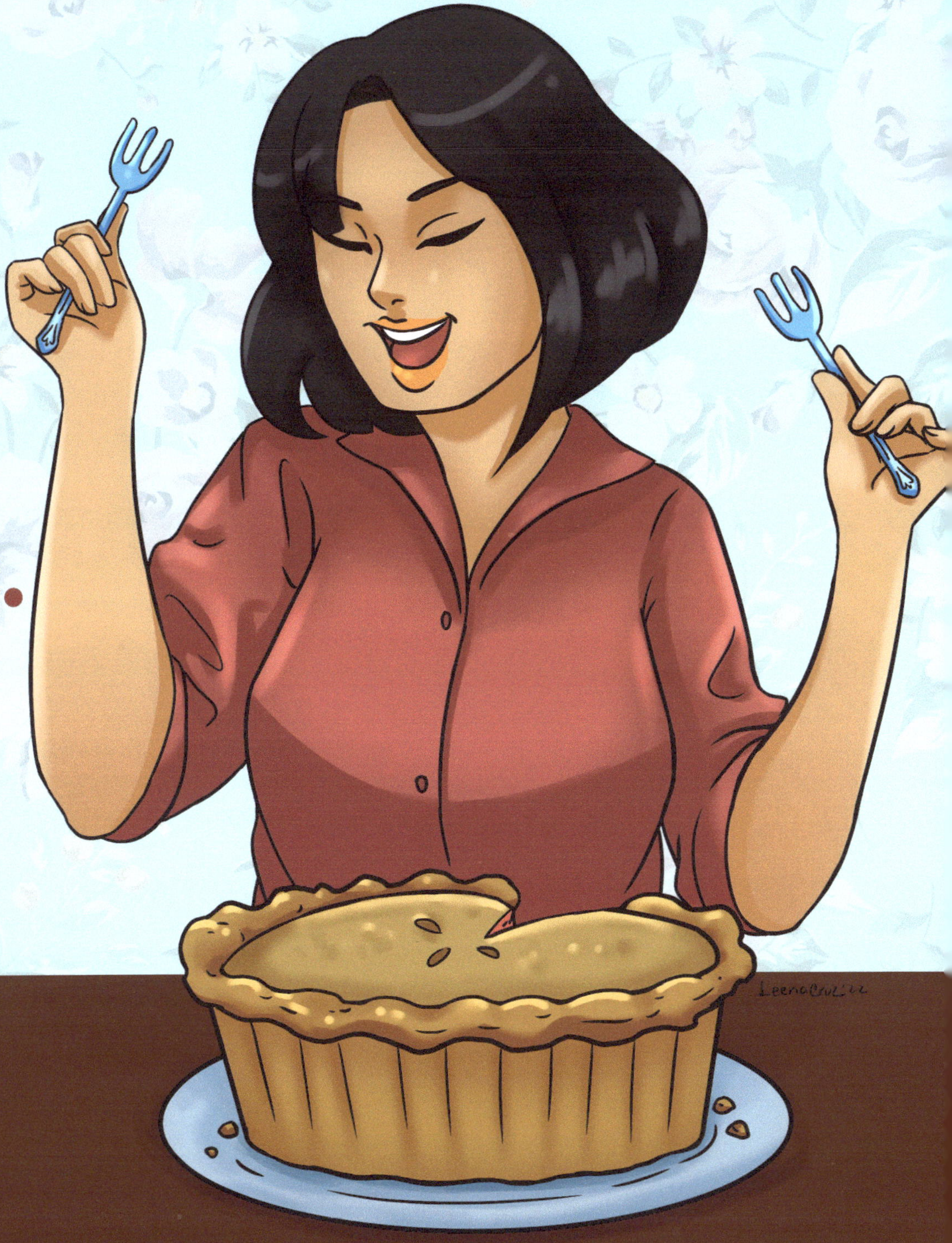

Oh, hey there, gray hair.
What the heck
are you doing there?

Have you come
to party with your friends?

I could try plucking,
but then
we already know
how this game ends.

Fuck you,
I'm 50.
Time for
Miss Clairol
again.

How's it hanging,
boobs and butt?
I see you
heading that direction.

I know gravity
is a bitch.
I already gave up
on perfection.

I threw away my underwire, and I know there's no magic pill.

Then and Now Challenge

Actual images of the author

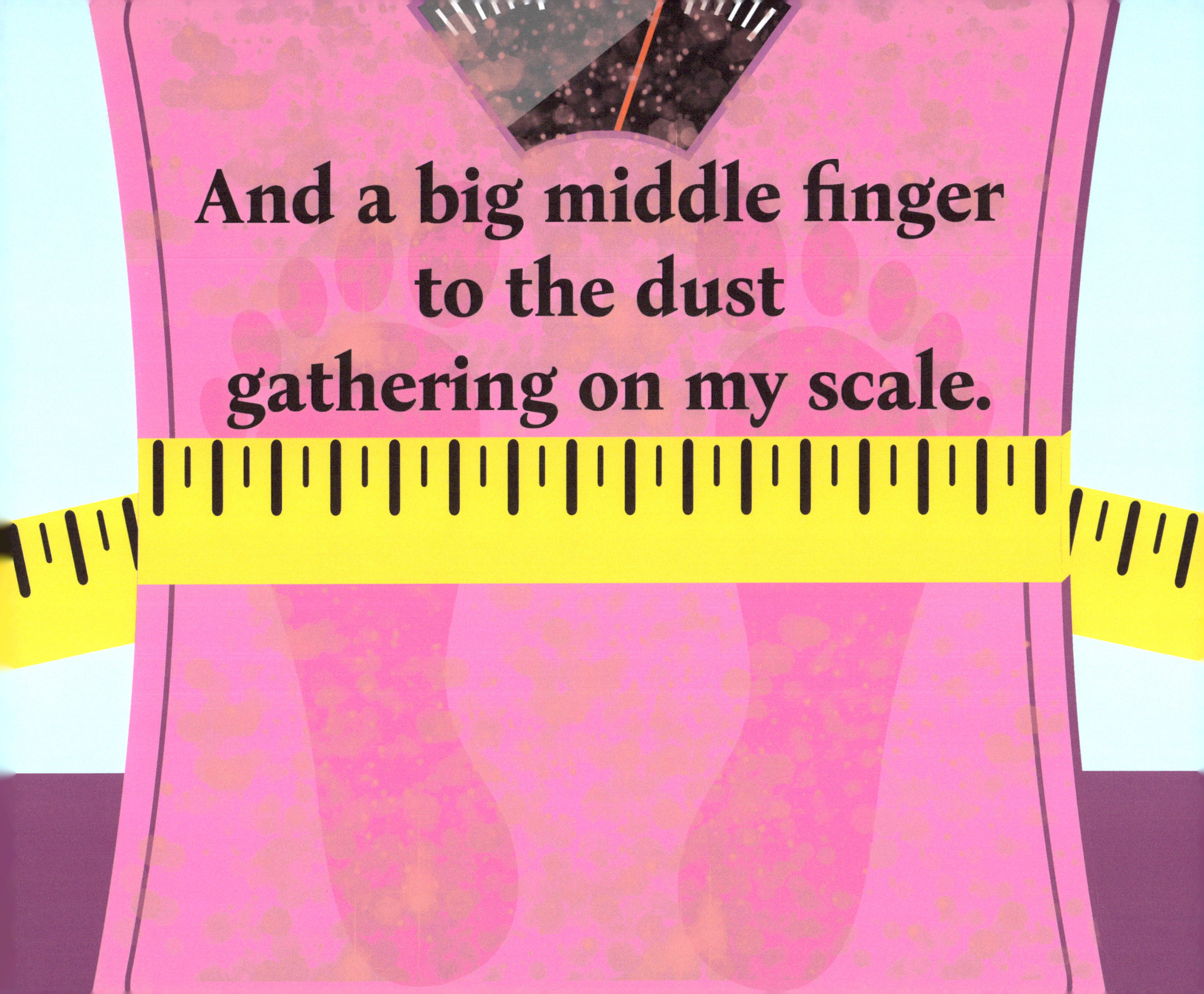

And a big middle finger to the dust gathering on my scale.

What the hell, hormones, unbalanced and unhinged? My thyroid took a holiday, and my ovaries went on a binge.

SEND MORE WINE

Now it's pills
in the morning
and creams
at night...

Boob-sweat
and bellyaches,
but I'm not
giving up the fight.
So before you think
these setbacks
will own me...

Fuck off, hot flashes. I'm tougher than that, even at fabulous 50.

Hey, body parts,
you've lost your smarts.
I never told you
to quit working.

You give new meaning to what the kids call twerking.

My gallbladder threw a fit.
My knee went on a bender.
My transmission took a shit,
and I think I broke my fender.

If I could give you
a middle finger,
I'd add an extender.

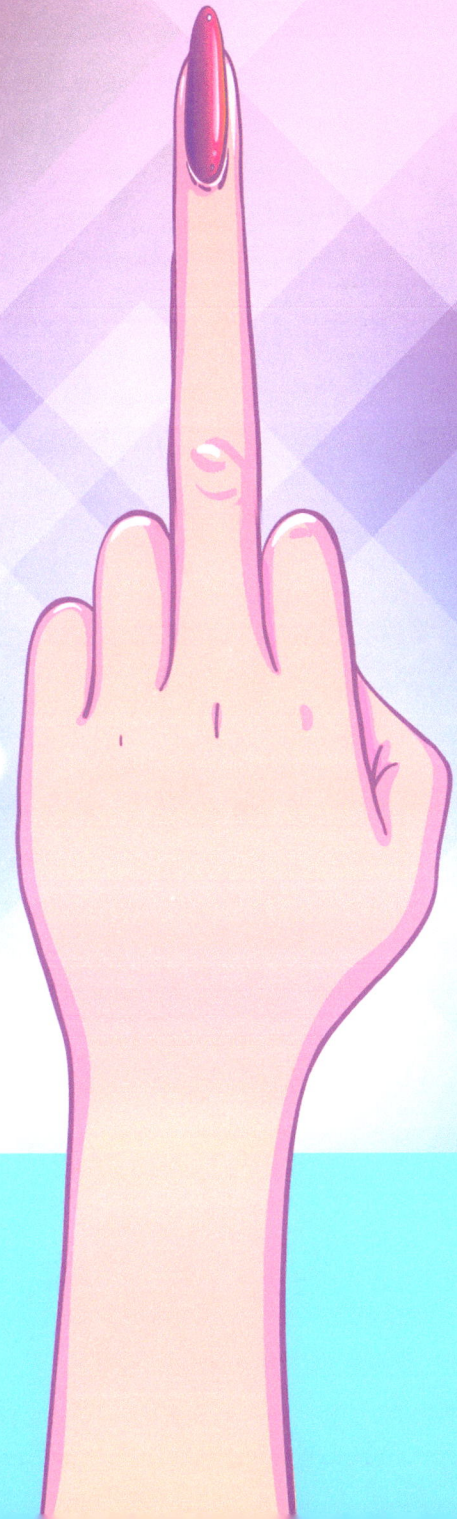

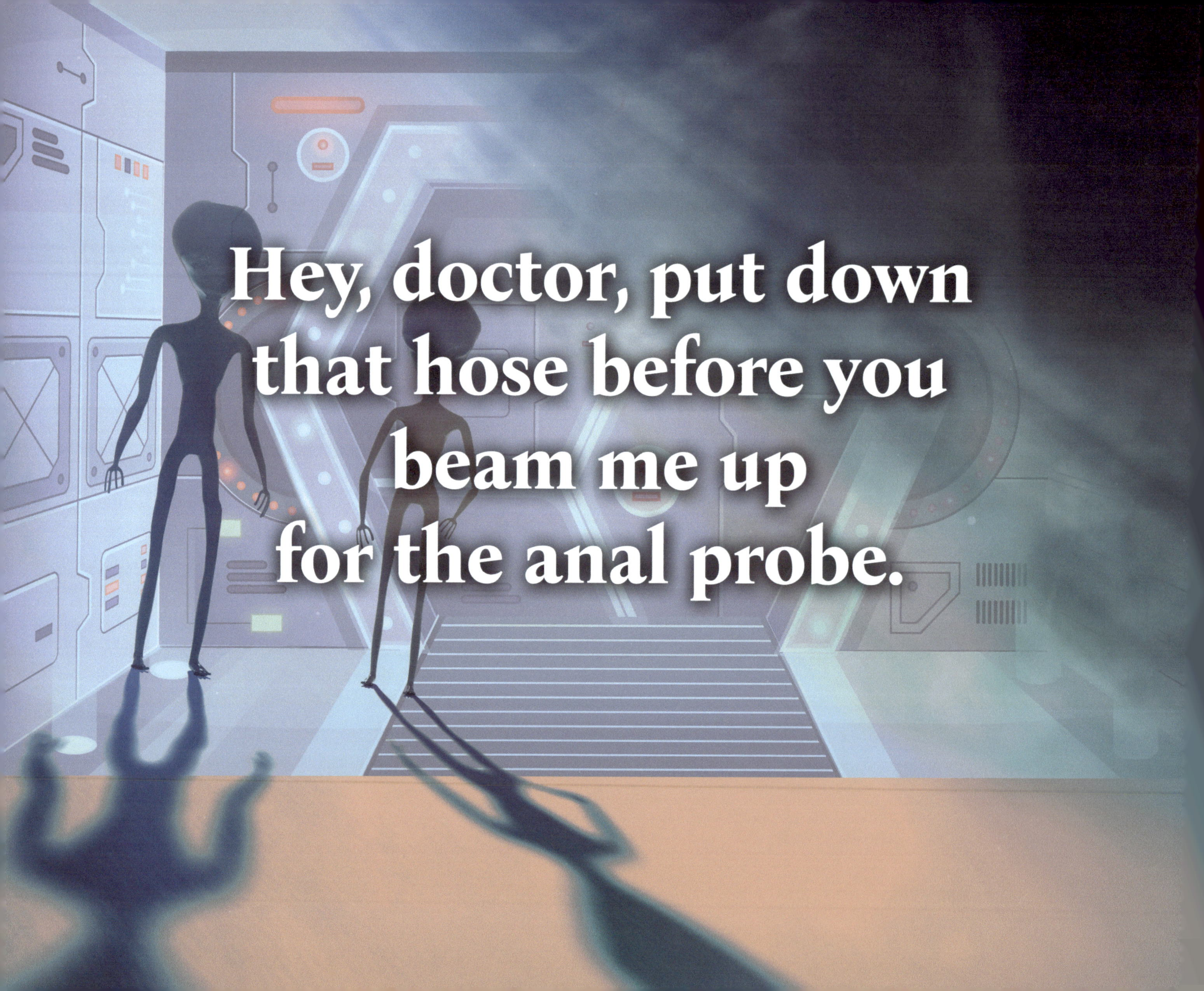

Hey, doctor, put down
that hose before you
beam me up
for the anal probe.

I know it's
not as bad
as I think,
but shouldn't
you first
buy me a drink?

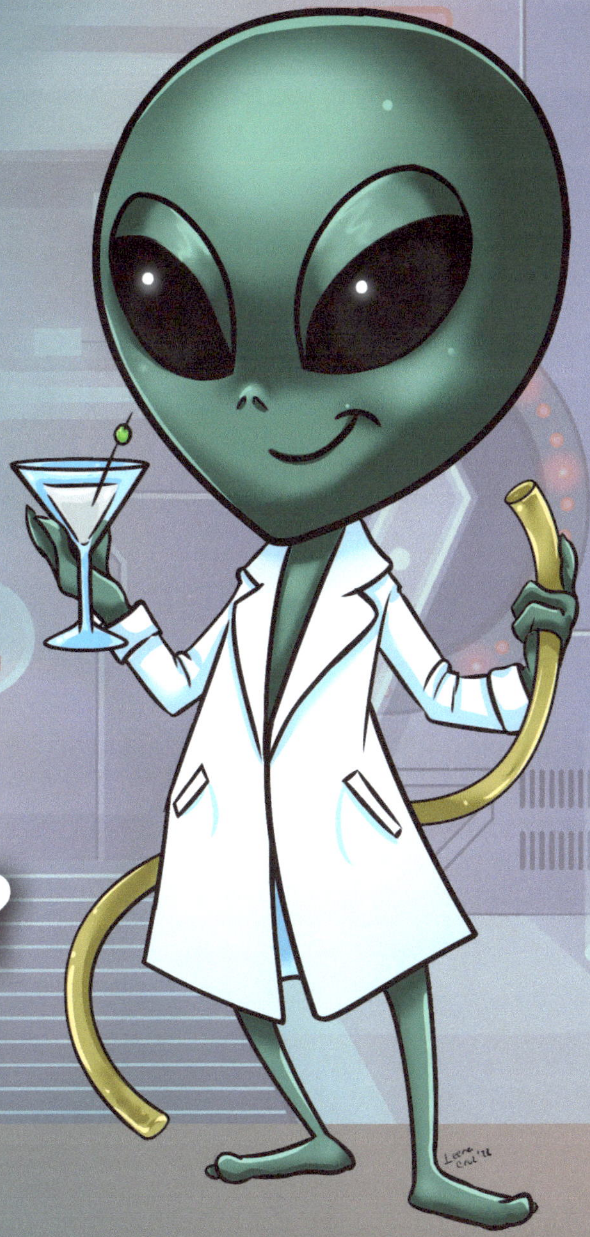

And haven't my boobies been tortured enough?

Mammogram,
slam-o-gram,
what the fuck?

Back off, chin hair.
What do you
think you're doing?
I told you not to grow there,
but like damn weeds
you're blooming.

I need to spend more time managing my grooming.

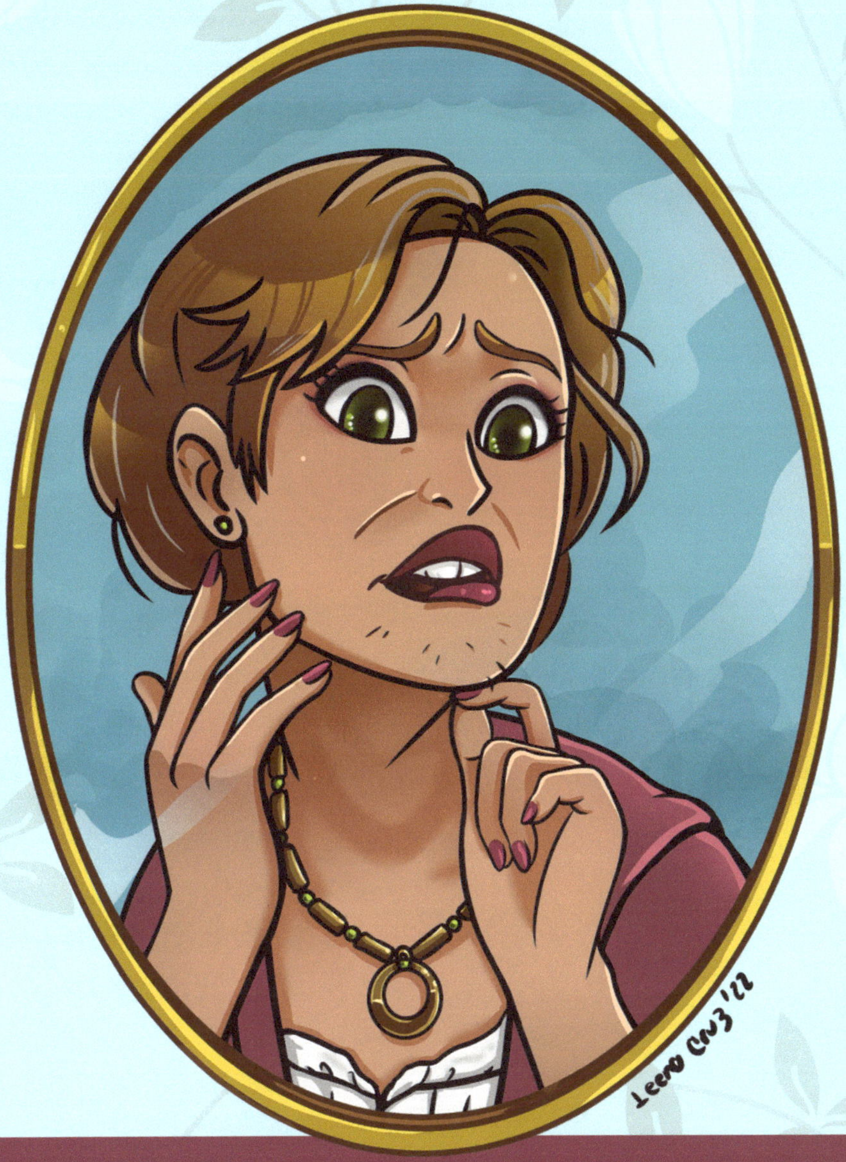

HAPPY BIRTHDAY

Goodbye wax, bleach, and tweezers. Hello chocolate, wine, and razors.

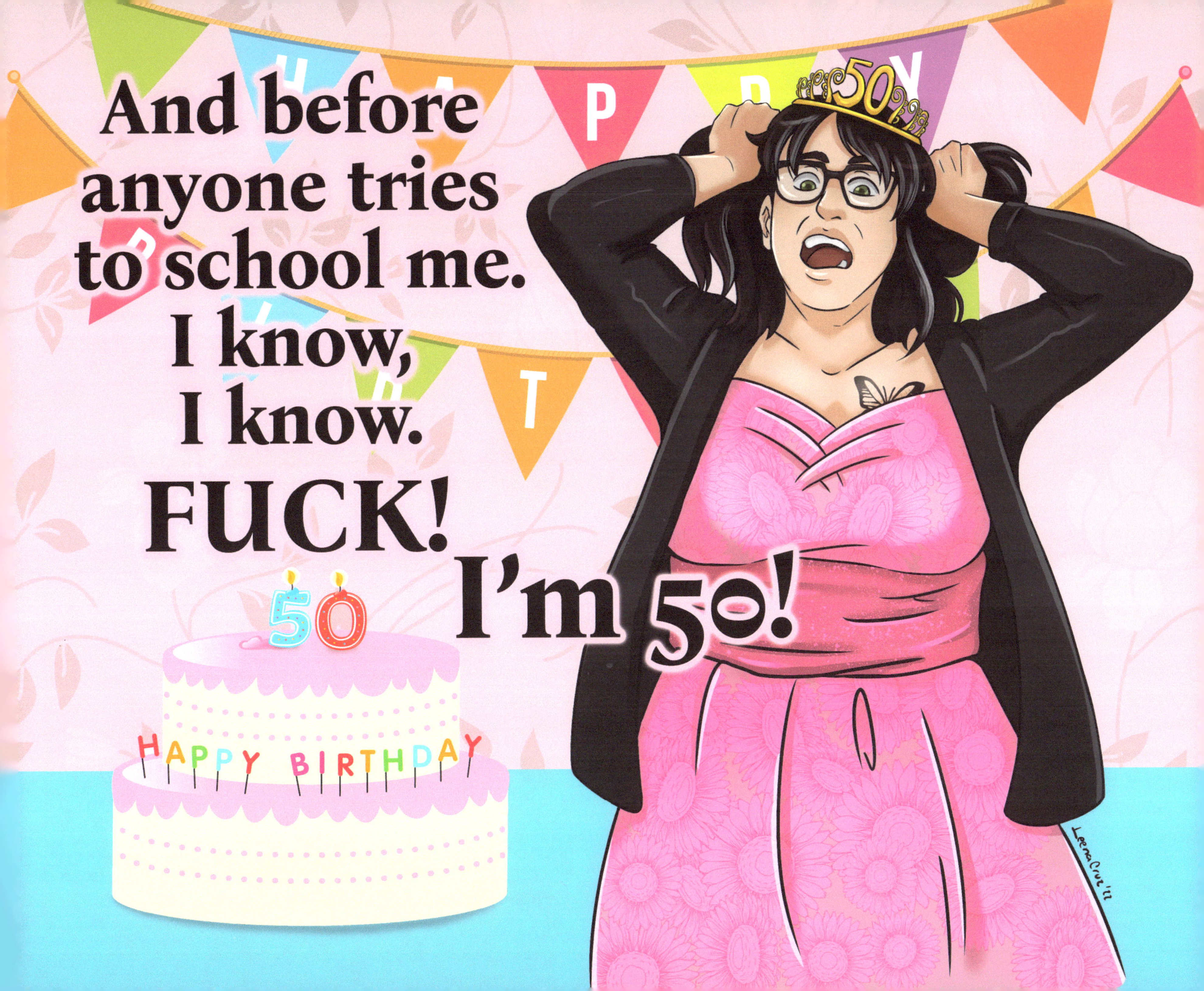
And before anyone tries to school me.
I know, I know.
FUCK!
I'm 50!
50
HAPPY BIRTHDAY
50

A message from Tara West...

Congratulations! You've made it to the end of the book. I'm assuming you liked it. Maybe loved it? If so, mind popping by wherever you purchased this book and leaving a review? It's how indie authors like me stay in business. If you didn't like it, do yourself a favor and go to the toilet and pull that stick out of your ass. There. Doesn't that feel better?

"So who is this author?" You're probably wondering. Or maybe you don't give two shits. In which case, it's a good time to close the book. This is the part where I droll on about my life. In case you haven't guessed already, I just turned 50. That's right, I'm quintessential Gen X.

After I got off the school bus, I let myself in our house, made a grilled cheese (real butter on both sides), and vegged out on MTV. I made out with my Simon LeBon poster at least a dozen times a week. (His poor lips were so crusty!) I knew when all my friends were on their periods by the smell of their maxi pads wafting across the room. I used way too much Aqua Net and spent an hour every morning teasing my hair until it could almost scrape the ceiling. I thought I could dance like Jennifer Beals in Flashdance, but I probably looked like an epileptic chicken. I loved slumber parties with my friends. We made prank calls and stayed up all night watching scary movies like The Exorcist and Jaws, which in turn made it nearly impossible for me to sleep or go swimming. I got my first job in fast food and my second selling Levi jeans.

I worked (and partied) all through college. At some point, I think I got a degree in English, but my memory is a bit fuzzy. I blame all the sorority socials, all-nighter study sessions, and Jolt Colas. I married my sweetheart. We were poor. Our cars broke down a lot. This was before cell phones. Fun times. We ate a lot of macaroni and cheese and lived in a military base single-wide trailer with a swamp cooler that was always on the fritz. We survived (and we're still in love.) I spent eight agonizing...eh blissful years as a high school English teacher. Are you bored yet? I'll try to speed things up. Fans of my romance novels get a much shorter version of my life, so consider yourself lucky! Oh, yeah. I'm a *USA Today* Bestselling novelist of paranormal and fantasy romance. I'll get to that later. Sheesh!

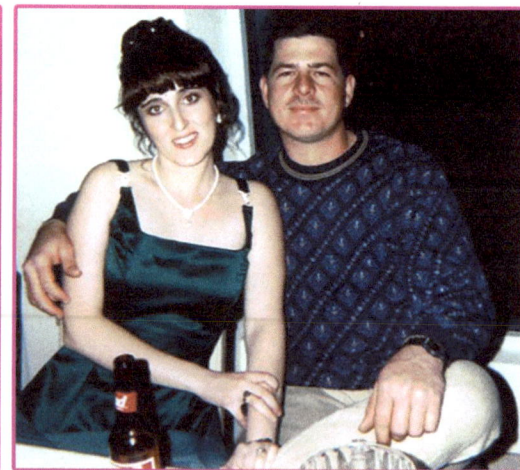

Hubs got a civilian job, and I quit teaching to stay home with my baby girl, and then I got sick. Real sick. Thought-I-was-dying-sick. Spent thousands of dollars and too many good years of my life trying to figure myself out thanks to clueless doctors. But that's a whole 'nother book! So Dr. Google helped diagnose me with thyroid and Celiac disease, and life is much better now that I've taken control of my health. My friends and I created the largest autoimmune thyroid support group in the world, Hashimoto's 411, (just so I don't get hundreds of emails asking.) I avoid gluten or else I turn into Godzilla (but the flames come out the other end.) My romance books started selling, and we moved into my dream house. Life was going great until I lost my mom to Alzheimer's and my dear cousin Bam to breast cancer. Bam was just 47.

On a happier note, I have rabbits. Oh, I didn't mention the rabbits, did I? Yeah, I'm the crazy rabbit lady. You didn't expect the author of a book with so many F words to not be at least a little batshit, did you? I have four of my own fluffy thumpers, and I have had up to seven other rabbits while fostering for our local rescue. They make life so much fun, even though one is currently throwing her food bowl while I'm trying to write this. I also have one blind dog, one yappy dog, and one woofy dog. When I'm not baby talking to my animals and driving my teen nuts, hubs and I love to give ourselves neck cramps on our mid-life crisis jet skis out in the Texas Hill Country.

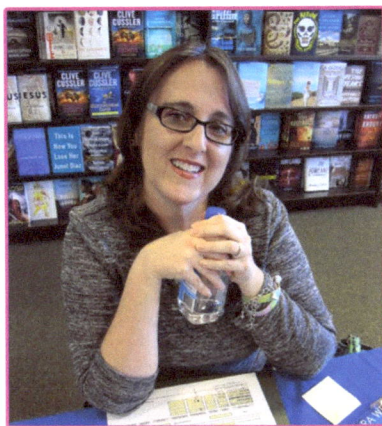

Oh, yeah. I still haven't told you about my other books. I write books with lots of smutty shifter sex. My Hungry for Her Wolves Series is my most popular. I also have a hilarious, steamy fallen angel series called Eternally Yours. Book one is Divine and Dateless, and I promise you'll squee yourself with laughter. I also have a new funny and sexy PNR series with MCs over age 40 coming out fall 2022. Book one is called Sugar, Spice, and Magical Midlife. Plus, another rip snortin' book like this one called F**king After 50. Be looking for them! I have over 40 published novels, so you're sure to find one that suits your taste. Also check out my crude parody penname, PJ Jones.

And now you're probably wondering what the hell was I thinking when I wrote this book. I went into my thirties and forties kicking and screaming. Then one day I woke up and said, "Holy shit! I got old! When did that happen?" So here I am at fabulous fifty, and it doesn't feel half bad. I made it when others didn't. Why not celebrate with a fun new book? I've earned that privilege. And to anyone who says otherwise, kindly refer to the first two words in the title of my book.

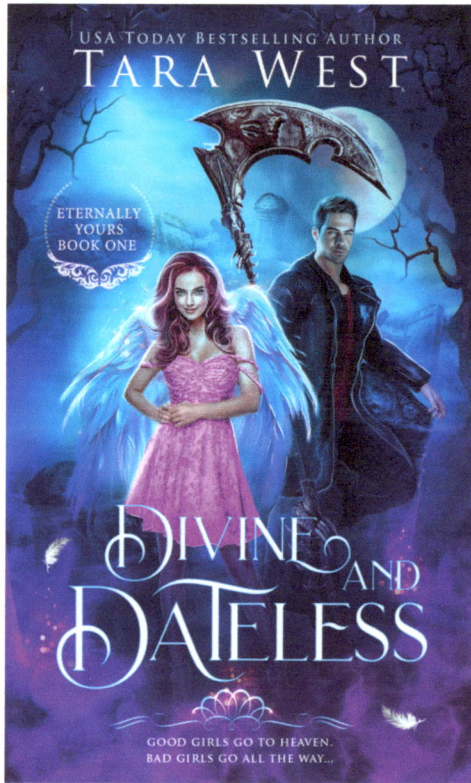

Other Books by Tara West

Eternally Yours
Divine and Dateless
Damned and Desirable
Damned and Desperate
Demonic and Deserted
Dead and Delicious

Dawn of the Dragon Queen
Dragon Song
Dragon Storm

Hungry for Her Wolves
Hungry for Her Wolves
Longing for Her Wolves
Desperate for Her Wolves
Tempted by Her Wolves
Fighting for Her Wolves
Fated for Her Wolves
Defending Her Wolves
Saving Her Wolves
Hungry for Her Demon Wolves
Captured by Her Demon Wolves
Hunted by Her Demon Wolves

Dragon Defenders
The Fae Queen's Warriors
The Fae Queen's Captors
The Fae Queen's Saviors

F**k Off, I'm 50
F**king After 50 (releasing fall 2022)

For more of my published works, visit www.tarawest.com, facebook.com/tarawestauthor, or my Amazon page. I love to hear from my readers at tarawestauthor@gmail.com. I also have a few comedies under the name PJ Jones such as Romance Novel (a rip-snortin' parody of Twilight and just about every romance trope) and Driving Me Nuts (three mental patients, two loaded guns, one stolen car, and a whole lot of trouble.) If you decide to look up those books, be warned, I'm not responsible for bleeding eyeballs!

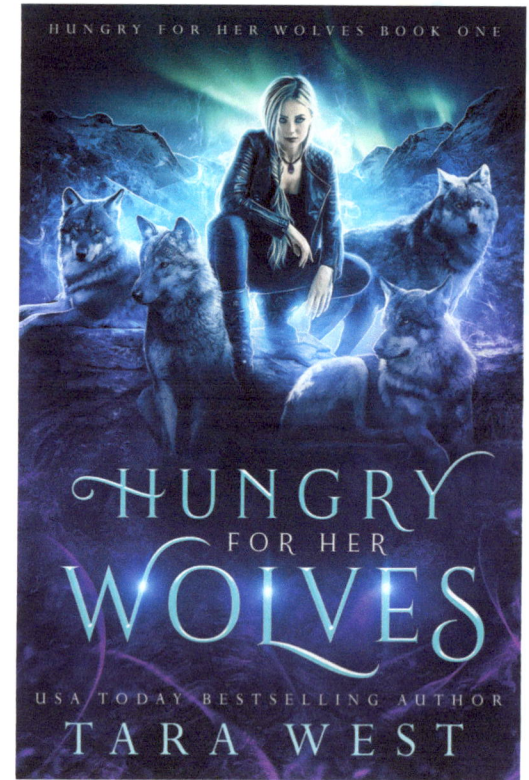

A Message From Leena Cruz

Hi! Thank you for reading this far! I am illustrator Leena Cruz and hope you enjoy the images I came up with as much as I enjoyed drawing them. Tara is a wonderful author, and her ideas were so fun to draw. She gave me the exact dose of direction, creative freedom, and trust to create the art you saw. When she told me the premise of the book, I was immediately in! A feminine view about turning 50 and its challenges? Hell yeah! I wanted to illustrate that.

I had worked on children's books, board games, indie videogames, and graphic design in general since I graduated from graphic design, but this was the first time I illustrated a fun book for women reaching 50, and honestly, it was hilarious.

Right now, I am expanding my work to book covers and art for other genres. I love to create art for board games, and I have been working on two projects that are almost ready to publish (hope I can talk about it soon). I enjoy creating characters, scenes, and props for these projects, giving logic and life to those fantastic worlds and games. Concept art, they call it.

When I'm not creating, eating, or sleeping, I like to play videogames, read, watch horror movies, enjoy life with my family, go out with my friends, walk by the beach or the valley, play board games, RPGS or creating plushies. I love to sew and construct things. Creating plushies is my new hobby, so my house is full of fabrics and patterns now.

If you want to see more of my art please visit my website @
www.leenacruz.com or follow me on my social media @
IG @leencruzart and
FB @leenacruzart

And if you need help with your creative project, contact me!
All the best,
Leena

Shameless author humbly requesting
you go to wherever you purchased
this book and leave a review.
More reviews help readers find
my books and help indie
authors like me make a living.

Please spread the word about my books
on your social media sites,
so I don't have to get a real job.
THANKS!!!

www.ingramcontent.com/pod-product-compliance
Lightning Source LLC
Chambersburg PA
CBHW042108090426

42811CB00018B/1886